Organization

Each of the four units contains a variety of lessons and activities that correlate to specific standards for the second grade in the areas of reading, math, science, and social studies.

- **Reading:** The lessons in the reading section are designed to address most of the standards for language arts. The activities provide graphic organizers and lessons that allow the students to read and understand a variety of materials, to respond to literature in various ways, to use literary terminology, and to use comprehension strategies such as sequencing, finding main idea, identifying cause and effect, and summarizing. These lessons and activities can be modified to reach multiple intelligences.

- **Math:** The lessons in the math section are designed to address several of the math standards for second grade. They provide the opportunity for the students to identify patterns, skip-count, and use charts and calendars. The students will also identify shapes, estimate lengths, and practice using fractions.

- **Science:** In addressing the standards, these lessons allow the students to understand the purpose of scientific investigations, ask questions, state predictions, make observations, give reasonable explanations for data collected, use the data to make tables and charts, and organize observations in written form.

- **Social Studies:** The lessons in this section are designed to address several standards for second-grade social studies. They encourage students to observe the relationships between different students' birthdays, to learn more about their community, and to practice basic map skills.

Standards

This is a list of the standards adapted into the lesson plans and activities used, although not all of them are represented in this book.

Reading:
- Sort words according to similarities in structure
- Identify elements in a story, including characters, setting, events, problem, and solution
- Apply thinking skills to reading, writing, speaking, listening, and viewing
- Summarize information from a story
- Identify the cause and the effect
- Identify the main idea and important details of a passage

Math:
- Recognize, identify, and apply patterns in number series
- Interpret tables to solve problems
- Skip-count in multiples of twos, threes, and fives
- Read, interpret, and apply information from a calendar to solve problems
- Estimate measurement and correctly identify an appropriate tool for measuring
- Identify the relationships of pictures and their fractions
- Identify shapes in real world situations and categorize them based on attributes

Science:
- Organize and classify items according to their states of matter
- Predict and observe weather patterns
- Label, examine, and analyze information about fossils
- Observe the relationship between the Sun and shadows
- Categorize rocks according to their composition

Social Studies:
- Use a graphic organizer to examine important people, businesses, and attributes of the students' community
- Sequence events on a time line
- Develop map reading skills and identify parts of a map

Lesson Plans Using Graphic Organizers, Grade 2

Table of Contents

Introduction

What is a good education? There are many different answers to that question and differences of opinion regarding what a good education is. One way that states decided to clarify this question was by developing educational standards. These standards detail what students should know and be able to do in each subject area at a given grade level. Standards are high and consistent expectations for all students.

Teachers use classroom activities and assessments to determine if students are meeting or exceeding established standards. With a heavy emphasis being placed on these assessments and the adoption of these standards, the focus of education becomes not just what teachers teach but also what students learn. Teachers must focus their classroom efforts on students' meeting and exceeding standards.

Because there is such strong emphasis placed on these standards and assessments, teachers are in need of lessons and graphic organizers that they can use to ensure that they are covering the standards. The purpose of this book is to provide detailed lessons in correlation to the standards listed in Steck-Vaughn's *Parents' Guide to Standards* (ISBN 0-8172-6184-2) using Madeline Hunter's model of anticipatory set, purpose, input, modeling, guided practice, checking for understanding, independent practice, and closure. These steps provide an effective model for enhancing and maximizing learning:

- Anticipatory set: a short activity to focus the students' attention before the actual lesson begins
- Purpose: the reason the students need to learn the skill
- Input: the things the students need to be familiar with in order to understand the skill successfully (i.e., vocabulary words, concepts, etc.)
- Modeling: what the teacher shows in graphic form or what the finished product will look like
- Guided practice: the teacher leading the students through the necessary steps to perform the skill
- Check for understanding: the teacher asking questions to determine if the students understand the skill and can apply it independently
- Independent practice: the students working independently to apply the new skill
- Closure: the wrapup of the lesson

Each lesson consists of a lesson plan, a model, and reproducible practice and individual activities. Each lesson also contains a graphic organizer as a teaching and learning tool for each skill. These tools can be applied to other activities and are interchangeable across the curriculum. These lessons provide a resource to begin implementing the standards and ensuring students' mastery of these skills.

Dear Parent,

To ensure that your child has a successful year and meets the requirements to advance to the next grade, our district has developed standards that each child must master. I focus my lessons on those skills listed in each standard to make sure your child receives the proper instruction for those skills. During this school year, our class will be working with activities in reading, mathematics, science, and social studies. We will be completing activities that provide practice to ensure mastery of these important skills. You can play an active role in your child's education. There are many things that you can do to help your child gain a good education.

From time to time I may send home activity sheets. To help your child, please consider the following suggestions:

- Provide a quiet place for your child to study or do homework. Make sure your child has all the supplies necessary to complete the work.
- Set a time for your child to study or do homework. This will help your child manage his or her time better.
- Go over the activity's directions together. Make sure your child knows what he or she is supposed to do.
- Give help when needed, but remember that the activity is your child's responsibility.
- Check the activity when it is done. Go over any parts your child may have had trouble completing.
- Help your child study for tests by asking sample questions or going over the material to be covered.
- Review all of the work your child brings home, and note improvements as well as activities that need reviewing.

Together we can help your child maintain a positive attitude about the activities while ensuring academic growth and success. Let your child know that each activity provides an opportunity to have fun and to learn. Above all, enjoy this time you spend with your child. He or she will feel your support, and skills will improve with each activity's completion!

Thank you for your help!

Cordially,

List of Graphic Organizers

Tool 1 Sorting Rhyming Words

Preparation: Make copies of pages 8, 9, and 10 for the students. Make overheads of pages 8 and 9.

Anticipatory Set: Say two sets of words, and ask the students to tell you which set of words has the same ending sound. Say the words *see* and *tree*. Ask if they have the same ending sounds. Then say the words *dog* and *day*. Ask if they have the same ending sounds.

Purpose: Explain to the students that they will be looking for words that rhyme in a poem. Tell the students that they are going to sort words by pairing them if they rhyme.

Input: Define *rhymes* as words that have the same ending sounds and that sound the same.

Modeling: Place the poem on page 8 on the overhead. Ask the students to make observations about the poem. Ask what they notice about the lines, title, and punctuation. Ask them if this work looks like the stories they see in books. Explain that this is a poem, and identify the lines and the title. Have students tell you how many lines there are. Then, tell the students to listen as you read the poem. They are to listen for words that sound the same. After reading the poem, place page 9 on the overhead. Explain the directions. With the students, look at the words at the bottom of the poem on page 8. Pick one word and read it to the students. Ask them which word rhymes with that word. Then put the pair in the first box on page 9.

Guided Practice: Divide the students into partners. Pass out pages 8 and 9. Have the partners cut out the words and sort them into the boxes. They will only use the first five boxes. Don't have them glue the words down. They will use page 9 for another poem.

Check for Understanding: After the students have completed their partner work, review the definition of rhyming. Ask several students to name the pairs of rhyming words that they found. Place those words into the boxes on the overhead so the students can check their work.

Independent Practice: Pass out page 10. Read the poem. Have the students listen to the first reading and read along with you on the second reading. Point to the words at the bottom of the page. Explain that they are going to use the words to find pairs of words that rhyme. After they put two words in each box on page 9, they can glue them down.

Closure: Review what it means to rhyme. Ask for students to give you examples of words that rhyme. Then say a word, and have students think of words that rhyme with it. You can write them down or do this orally.

Name _____   Date _____

The Swing

Robert Louis Stevenson

How do you like to go up in a swing,
Up in the air so blue?
Oh, I do think it the pleasantest thing
Ever a child can do!
Up in the air and over the wall,
Till I can see so wide,
Rivers and trees and cattle and all
Over the countryside—
Till I look down on the garden green
Down on the roof so brown—
Up in the air I go flying again,
Up in the air and down!
How do you like to go up in a swing,
Up in the air so blue?
Oh, I do think it the pleasantest thing
Ever a child can do!

countryside	thing	all	brown	do
blue	wide	down	swing	wall

Name _____   Date _____

Rhyming Pairs

Directions

Read the poem. Cut out the words below the poem. Match the
words that rhyme. Glue each set of rhyming words in a box.

1.

5.

2.

6.

3.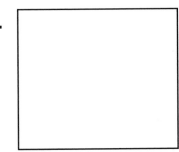

7.

4.

The Star

Jane Taylor

Twinkle, twinkle, little star,
How I wonder what you are!
Up above the world so high,
Like a diamond in the sky.
When the blazing Sun is gone,
When it nothing shines upon,
Then you show your little light,
Twinkle, twinkle, all the night.
Then the traveler in the dark,
Thanks you for your tiny spark;
He could not see which way to go,
If you did not twinkle so.
In the dark blue sky you keep,
And often through my curtains peep,
For you never shut your eye,
Till the Sun is in the sky.
As your bright and tiny spark
Lights the traveler in the dark—
Though I know not what you are,
Twinkle, twinkle, little star.

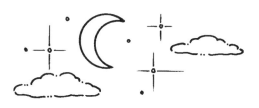

star	so	gone	keep	go
upon	light	sky	dark	spark
night	are	peep	eye	

Unit 1: Reading

Lesson Plans Using Graphic Organizers 2, SV 2070-2

Tool 2 Using a Story Map

Prepare: Make copies of pages 13 (two sets) and 14 for students. Make overheads of pages 12 and 13. Write the five story elements and their definitions on sentence strips, and put the strips in a pocket chart.

Anticipatory Set: Ask the students to tell you things that every good story must have. When a student says a story element, turn its strip around. After the students have mentioned the five story elements, ask them why these are important. Would a story make sense without characters? Without a setting?

Purpose: Explain that the students will identify the five elements in a fiction story.

Input: Review the definition of *fiction*—a made-up or fantasy story—and the definitions of the five story elements: *characters*, *setting*, *problem*, *events*, and *solution*.

Modeling: Place page 12 on the overhead. Read the passage out loud. Then place page 13 on the overhead. Point to the five different story elements on the page. Then ask the students to remember the story. Ask them to identify the characters in the story. If needed, review the definition of *character*. Then ask the students to identify a setting. Explain that the students are now going to complete the chart for this story with a partner. Review the definitions of *events*, *problem*, and *solution*.

Guided Practice: Divide the class into partners. Pass out page 13 to the partners. Have one student write. Both students will work together to complete the story map. Leave the passage on the overhead. Monitor the students as they work.

Check for Understanding: Refocus the group on the overhead. Ask the students to volunteer answers for the events, problem, and solution. Discuss the story elements and the students' answers.

Independent Practice: Pass out page 14 and another page 13 for independent work. Explain that the students will complete the chart using the passage. Review quickly the five story elements and their definitions. Monitor the students as they complete the map.

Closure: Review why the five story elements are important. Cover them up on the board and have students volunteer to list and define the five story elements. Have the students choose a book for themselves. While they are reading, they should note the different story elements.

A New Baby

Segi's parents were very happy. Segi's mother was going to have a baby. Segi's father said Segi would love being a big sister. Segi was not so sure.

Segi's parents were excited. They spent a lot of time getting ready. They turned one room into a baby room. They got the baby crib from the attic. Segi's friends had ideas about babies. "Babies take lots of time," said Tina. "What if your mom and dad don't have time left for you?"

"Mothers get tired with new babies," said Mimi. "They take lots of energy. Your mom won't want to play games with you." This did not sound good to Segi.

Segi watched her mother's stomach. It got bigger and bigger. Soon the baby would arrive. One night, Segi began to cry. She told her mother what her friends had said. Segi didn't want a new baby. Her mother held her. "Segi," she said, "you will always be very special. It won't matter how many babies we have."

Segi's mother went to the hospital. Two days later, she brought home a baby boy. Segi thought he was a beautiful baby. Her father lifted her up for a better look. Segi said, "Hi, little brother. I'm your big sister, Segi!"

Name _____ Date _____

Story Map

Title: _____

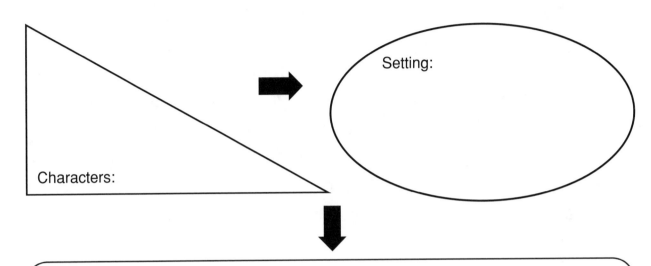

Characters:

Setting:

Problem:

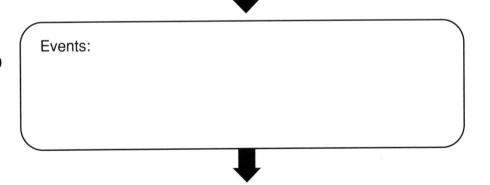

Events:

Solution:

Emma's Horse

Emma loved all the beautiful horses. She especially loved the little white horse with the tan spots and mane. She had secretly named her Belle. Emma's father did not like to name the horses. "Those horses are business, Emma, not pets," he would say. Besides, he thought she was still too young to take care of a horse. She knew she could do it. But she had to convince her father.

One morning Emma woke earlier than usual. She looked out the window. She could not see the horses. She dressed quickly and ran outside. Emma quickly discovered that the fence had been broken. All the horses had escaped! She ran back to the house to tell her father. He was on the telephone to his help. "Get over here quick," he said. "If those horses get past the river, we may never find them."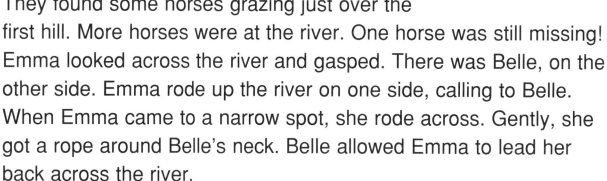

Emma's father agreed to let Emma help. They found some horses grazing just over the first hill. More horses were at the river. One horse was still missing! Emma looked across the river and gasped. There was Belle, on the other side. Emma rode up the river on one side, calling to Belle. When Emma came to a narrow spot, she rode across. Gently, she got a rope around Belle's neck. Belle allowed Emma to lead her back across the river.

When Emma's father realized what she had done, he was angry at first. She could have been hurt! But he knew she had a done a fine job.

"Emma, you worked hard enough to get that horse," said her father, smiling. "You may keep her."

(Tool 3) Predicting

Preparation: Write the five story elements and words from page 16 on sentence strips, cut them out, and put magnet tape on the back. Put the words in a pocket chart. Make copies of pages 16, 17, and 18 for the students, and make overheads of pages 17 and 18.

Anticipatory Set: Ask the students to help you think of the five elements that every good story must have. As the students say an element, have them define it. Put the elements on the board in this order: *Character, Setting, Problem, Events, Solution.*

Purpose: Explain that the lesson provides a review of story elements and practice predicting what a story will be about using story elements.

Input: Review the list of words. Familiarize students with the words, noting things such as if each is a name or a place or if it shows action.

Modeling: Explain that the students will categorize these words into the five elements from a story about which you have told them nothing. Model by using *Leona.* The best place for *Leona* would be under *Character* because it is a name. Place it in the *Character* column. Then choose a more difficult word like *canopy* to model. Remind the students that there are no wrong answers.

Guided Practice: Ask for one student to restate the instructions. Then, give each student a partner and a time limit of fifteen minutes to complete the chart. Monitor the partners as they work.

Check for Understanding: Call on partners to tell where they put each word and why. Write the words on the class chart. Emphasize that each group's chart will probably be different from the class chart.

Independent Practice: Now, explain that the next step will be to create a probable passage. Define *probable* as "probably," so the story will probably be right, or it will be close to the real story. Then, using the class chart, model how the students will write their own probable passage on the overhead of page 18. Model how to fill in the blanks, using each word in the columns to make complete sentences and checking them off. Explain that they will put all of the words under *Character* in the first blank in a complete sentence. Repeat for each section. Remind the students to use all of the words. The students will go to their seats and complete their own probable passage. Monitor the students to make sure they are on task.

Closure: Refocus on the class chart. Review the five story elements and why they are important. Ask three students to share their probable passages with the class. After they have read, ask the students if they want to know what the real story is about. Have them read it. Encourage them to note the differences between their passage and the real one. Invite the students to comment on how well they predicted the story.

Probable Passage Words

forest	Sun	Len Lizard	fell	branch
bird	Leona	canopy	safe	dropped
	wiser	amazing	down	

CHARACTER

SETTING

PROBLEM

EVENTS

SOLUTION

Probable Passage

The characters in this story are _____

_____.

The story takes place _____

_____.

The problem in the story is _____

_____

_____

_____.

Some things that happen in the story are _____

_____

_____

_____.

The problem is solved when _____

_____

_____

_____.

A Scare at the Top

Len Lizard lived deep in the forest. His best friend was Leona Lizard. Len and Leona played together in the leafy growth. They looked for bugs in the bark and under the leaves. They loved to feel the sunlight when it peeked in.

Len and Leona were curious. They wanted to see the canopy. It was high up in the forest. They had heard about its bright sunshine and the wonderful things to see. But it was no place for little lizards, their mothers said. Too many birds would love to snack on little Len and Leona!

Still, they were curious. So one day they sneaked to the top of a very large tree. The Sun felt warm and wonderful. They could see for miles. It was amazing! It was also very noisy. There were many birds with frightening cries. Suddenly, a bright yellow bird flew by and snatched Len from his branch. Leona screamed. Len struggled to get free. The yellow bird dropped Len. He fell down into the trees. His heart was fluttering in his body. But he was safe. Then he saw Leona. "Thank goodness you are all right!" cried Leona. "Let's get home. I'll never come back here again!"

"Yes," answered Len, "our mothers were right. This is no place for us!" They crawled quickly back down the tree. Len's body was sore where the bird's beak had held him. They reached home safely.

"Maybe," said Len, "we can go back again when we're older. We're already wiser!"

18

Tool 4 Sequencing

Preparation: Copy pages 20, 21, and 22 for students. Make overheads of pages 20 and 21.

Anticipatory Set: Ask the students to tell you the order in which they get dressed in the mornings. Have one student state the order, and have other students share how they do things differently. Listen for words like *first*, *next*, *then*, etc.

Purpose: Explain that when people do things like getting dressed, they usually have an order in which they do it. The order is called *sequence*. Explain that the students are going to be reading passages, and they are going to sequence the events in the stories.

Input: Define *sequence* as the order in which something happens. Review the definition of *events* as the things that happen in a story.

Modeling: Put page 20 on the overhead. Read the passage about Reed and Mandy. As you read, underline sequence words like *first* and *then*. After you read the passage, ask the students to tell you the first thing that happened in the story. Then, fill in the *Beginning* bubble on the sequence graphic organizer. Have the students identify the last thing that happened in the story, and fill in the *End* bubble.

Guided Practice: Now, explain that the students are going to fill in the events in the correct order that they happened in the middle of the passage. Divide the students into partners. Pass out page 20. Have the students reread the passage and use the passage to fill in the missing events in the correct order.

Check for Understanding: Refocus on the overhead. Ask the students to define *sequence*. Then reread the passage out loud, and ask for volunteers to give the events of the passage in order.

Independent Practice: Review sequencing, and explain the independent activity. Pass out pages 21 and 22. Explain that the students will read the passage, identify the first event, the last event, and the middle events in the correct sequence.

Closure: Review the definition of *sequencing*. Ask the students to think about things they do every day that they have to do in order. Ask them to think about how things would be if they did them in a different order.

Making Sandwiches

Reed went to Mandy's house for lunch. They made sandwiches. First, they got some bread. Mandy put lettuce and cheese on one slice of bread. Reed put some meat on another slice of bread. Then, they put the bread together. While Mandy poured some milk to drink, Reed got out the plates. They were ready to eat.

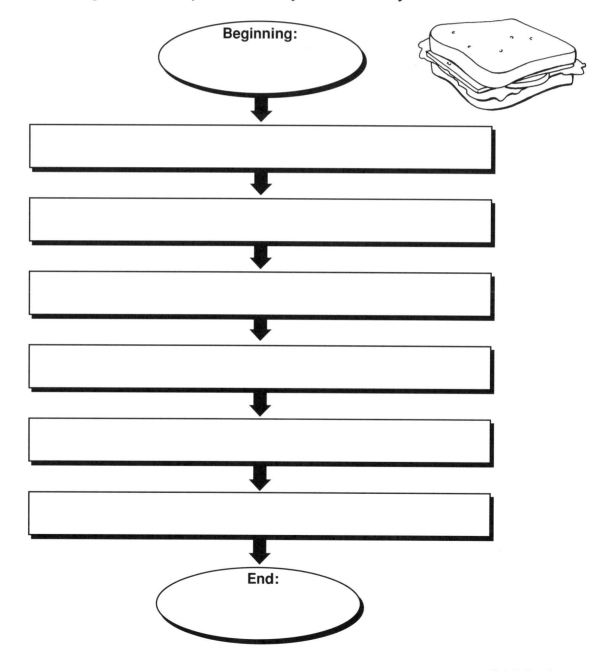

Peter and Jimmy

Peter likes his big brother, Jimmy.

One day, Jimmy comes home from school and says, "Come on, Peter, let's go outside and play ball." Peter is so excited! They race to see who can get to the tree in the yard first. Jimmy wins.

Then, Jimmy throws the ball to Peter. Peter tries to throw the ball back to Jimmy, but the ball rolls on the ground part of the way. Then, Jimmy shows Peter how to kick the ball across the yard. Peter likes this game because he can kick the ball almost as far as Jimmy can. They are having fun taking turns kicking the ball. Jimmy shows Peter how to kick the ball high in the air. The two brothers play together until it is time for Jimmy to do his homework.

Name _____ Date _____

Sequencing Flowchart

Title: _____

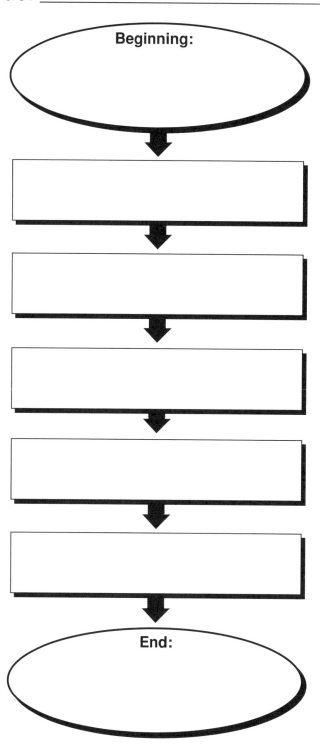

Beginning:

End:

Tool 5 Identifying Cause and Effect

Preparation: Copy pages 25 and 26 for the students. Make an overhead of page 24.

Anticipatory Set: Turn off the lights in your room. Ask what happened. Ask the students why it happened. Explain that the lights went off because you flipped the switch. Flipping the switch was the cause for the lights going out.

Purpose: Explain that things happen for a reason. They have a cause and an effect. Define *cause* and *effect*, and explain that the students are going to identify cause and effect in sentences.

Input: Define *cause* as the reason something happens and *effect* as what happens.

Modeling: Put page 24 on the overhead. Read the information out loud. Then, review the definitions of *cause* and *effect*. Have one student read the first sentence. Identify the effect. Write it in the bubble. Then, ask the students to identify why it happened. Tell them that this is the cause. Write it in the space. Repeat for the next sentence.

Guided Practice: Divide the students into partners. Pass out page 25. Have the students read the phrases. Tell them to cut out the boxes. Have them match each cause with each correct effect.

Check for Understanding: After a reasonable amount of time, ask the partners to look at the matches they made. Ask one student to state a cause and effect. Then, ask the rest of the students if they agree. Do this for all the pairs.

Independent Practice: Pass out page 26. Explain that the students will read the sentences and write the causes and effects in the boxes. Monitor the students as they work.

Closure: Review the definitions of *cause* and *effect*. Then, ask the students to provide a real world example of a cause and an effect. Have one student state an effect, and have another student suggest the cause. Tell the students to think about other subjects and situations that require the use of cause and effect.

Name _____ Date _____

I Wonder Why

What are a cause and an effect?

A <u>cause</u> is what makes something happen or why it happens. An <u>effect</u> is what happens. Read the following sentence. See if you can tell which is the <u>cause</u> and which is the <u>effect</u>.

Jill was happy because she got a puppy.

What is the effect? The effect is that Jill felt happy. What caused her to feel happy? The cause is that she got a puppy.

1. The cookies were gone because the children ate them all.

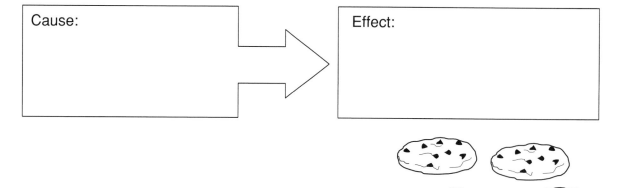

2. Billy's bike had a flat tire, so he had to walk home.

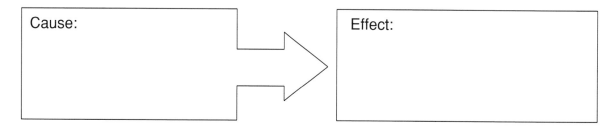

Matching Cause with Effect

Directions

Read the phrases. Cut out the boxes. Match the cause with the effect.

E: He stayed home from school	C: Emily raked the yard
E: The children could not play outside	C: Since it was Marie's birthday
E: The plant died	C: Jose was sick
E: She had a big cake	C: Because nobody watered it
E: She was given a dollar	C: Since it was raining

Finding the Cause and Effect

Directions

Read the sentence. Write the cause and the effect for each sentence in the box.

1. Jason and Chris were hot, so they jumped into the water.

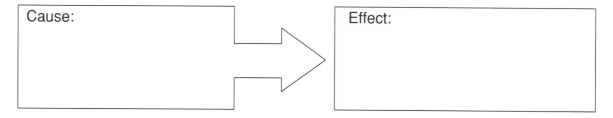

Cause: Effect:

2. Molly lost her pencil, so she had to buy another one.

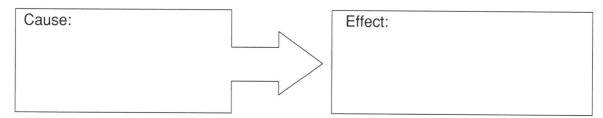

Cause: Effect:

3. Jenny fed her dog because it was hungry.

Cause: Effect:

4. The ice cream melted because Alex left it out on the table.

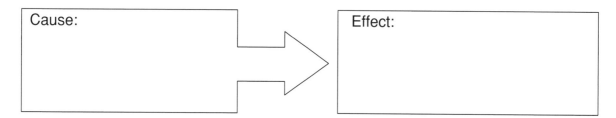

Cause: Effect:

Tool 6 Finding the Main Idea

Preparation: Make copies of pages 29 and 30. Make an overhead of page 28. Get a picture or poster of an event like a holiday, birthday, Olympics, etc.

Anticipatory Set: Ask the students to look at the poster. Have one student tell what the poster is mostly about in one sentence. Tell the students that the picture has a main purpose, and the student stated the main idea of the poster.

Purpose: Explain that the students are going to find the main idea of several passages.

Input: Define *main idea* as what the story is mostly about. The sentences that tell about the main idea are called *details*.

Modeling: Place page 28 on the overhead. Read the passage out loud, and ask the students if they can tell what it is mostly about. Write the response in the middle of the graphic organizer. Then, ask what sentences tell about the main idea. Write them in the surrounding boxes.

Guided Practice: Pass out page 29. Divide the students into groups. Have them read the paragraph and use the graphic organizer to find the main ideas and details of the paragraph. Monitor the students as they work.

Check for Understanding: Refocus the group, and ask one student to volunteer to tell the main idea of the paragraph. Then have the students explain which sentences are details. Have one student define *main idea* again.

Independent Practice: Pass out page 30. Read the paragraph out loud. Remind the students that they are going to tell what the paragraph is mostly about in the center box. Remind them that the details that tell about the main idea go around the box. Have the students reread the paragraph and complete the graphic organizer independently.

Closure: Review what the main idea and details are. Ask the students how finding the main idea can be applied to real world situations.

Identifying the Main Idea

Toys have been around for many years. The earliest toys were very simple. They were dolls and animal toys. They had no moving parts. Toys made today can have many moving parts. They are very different from the toys of the past!

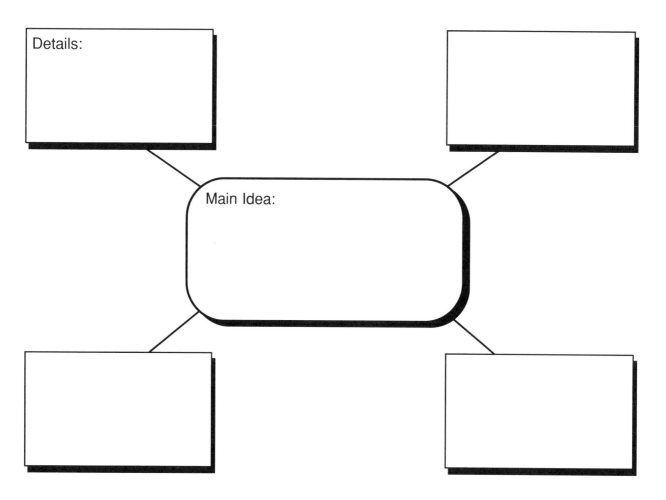

Details:

Main Idea:

28

Name _____   Date _____

Main Idea and Details

Directions

**Read the paragraph. Identify the main idea.
Fill in the chart.**

I love to go sliding in the snow. I like to skate on the ice. I like taking walks on snowy nights. I especially like sitting by a warm fire and reading a book on a winter evening. Winter is my favorite season of the year.

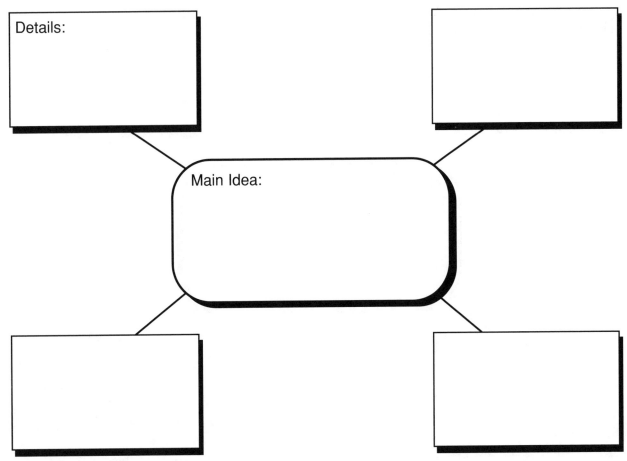

Details:

Main Idea:

More Main Idea and Details

Directions

Read the paragraph. Identify the main idea. Fill in the chart.

Terry is five years old. He thinks he is old enough to walk to school by himself. His mother is not so sure. She wants him to wait until he is six. Terry tries to remember all the safety rules. Every morning, he asks his mother whether he can walk to school by himself.

Details:

Main Idea:

Unit 1: Reading
Lesson Plans Using Graphic Organizers 2, SV 2070-2

(Tool 7) Summarizing

Preparation: Make copies of pages 33 and 34. Make overheads of pages 32 and 33. Make the letters *S*, *W*, *B*, and *S*, put magnetic strip tape on them, and put them on the board.

Anticipatory Set: Put the four letters, *SWBS*, on the board. Ask students to predict what they stand for. Then underneath each letter write: *S-somebody*, *W-wanted*, *B-but*, and *S-so*.

Purpose: Explain that the students are going to use these four letters to summarize a passage. The four letters are a part of a graphic organizer that will help them to summarize any story or passage.

Input: Define *summarizing* as highlighting the most important parts of a story or passage.

Modeling: Explain the model before you begin. Explain that the *S* is the somebody or main character in the story. The *W* is what the main character wants to do in the story. The *B* is the "but" or the problem in the story. And the *S* is the so, or the solution to how the character works out the problem. Place page 32 on the overhead. Read the passage. Then, put page 33 on the overhead. Ask the students to help you decide what to put under each column. Then, use the information in each column to write the summary sentence. The first blank is the character; after *wanted*, write what the character wanted; after *but*, write the problem; and after *so*, write how the problem is resolved. Then, review the process of the SWBS method of finding the summary.

Guided Practice: Divide the students into groups. Pass out pages 33 and 34 to the students. Explain that they will read the passage with their partners. Have them fill in the SWBS chart, but they should not complete the summary sentence. Monitor the students as they work.

Check for Understanding: Review what *SWBS* stands for. Show the model on the overhead again. Read the passage on page 34, and ask for volunteers to help you complete the SWBS for the passage.

Independent Practice: Explain that the students will now use the information they gathered with their partners to write the summary sentence. They will fill in the blanks and then reread the sentence to check if it makes sense.

Closure: Review what *SWBS* stands for. Ask the students to repeat *SWBS* three times to commit it to memory. Then review what the *S*, *W*, *B*, and *S* stand for. Ask students to think of other subjects or stories they can apply this model to for summarizing.

A Helping Hand

Robert watched his grandfather. He was moving boxes and tools around in the garage. Then, he began to sweep the dirt from the garage floor. Robert was getting impatient. He had already waited while his grandfather put away some groceries. His grandfather had told him that they could go fishing today. It would be their first fishing trip this year.

Robert could hardly wait to go. He could imagine how it would feel to cast his line into the water. He thought about how it felt when a fish took the bait. His line would tighten. The pole would bend a little. Then Robert would reel in the big one! But first, he had to wait for his grandfather. He had a lot of work to do.

Suddenly, Robert had an idea. He went to his grandfather and took the broom. He began to do the sweeping himself. His grandfather went back to moving the boxes. They finished cleaning the garage in no time. Then, Robert got a bucket full of soapy water. He and his grandfather soaped up the truck. Robert hosed off all the soap. The truck sparkled in the sunshine.

"Well, Robert!" said his grandfather. "With you helping me, my work went much faster! Now we have just one more thing to do."

Robert sighed. "What now?" he thought. "We will never go fishing!"

"We have to get our fishing poles and get going!" said his grandfather, laughing.

SWBS Graphic Organizer

Directions

Read the passage. Complete the chart. Use the information in the chart to write the summary.

S (somebody)	**W** (wanted)

B (but)	**S** (so)

Summary:

_____ wanted _____,

but _____

so _____ .

Peanut Pals

Maya held the peanut out to the little chipmunk. He scampered right over to her and took it. He put it into the pouch in his cheek along with the others.

Maya had seen the chipmunk on one of her first visits to the park. She always brought nuts with her, and each time she offered them to the chipmunk, he came closer and closer. Now, he was not at all afraid to take the treats that Maya brought. Maya named him Chip, and she loved to visit him.

One day Maya decided to bring Chip home. Then, she could see him all the time. He would be her pet. She bought a roomy cage and put soft wood curls on the bottom. She put in a little house. She put some nuts in the cage. Chip went to investigate the nuts in the cage. Maya closed the door and carried Chip home.

Soon Maya could see that Chip was not happy in his cage. She realized that Chip needed to be back in the park where he had a lot of room to play. Maya felt very sorry for taking Chip from his home. The next day, she carried the cage back to the park and set Chip free. He ran away quickly, and Maya thought she might never see him again. Still, she knew she had done the right thing.

Maya went back to the park a week later. She brought some nuts, but she did not expect to see Chip. He was probably afraid of her now, she thought. She sat on a bench and set out the peanuts. She began to read. Suddenly, she saw something moving. She turned to see her old friend Chip stuffing his face with the peanuts, just like always!

Tool 8 Identifying Patterns

Preparation: Make copies of pages 37 and 38 for students. Make an overhead of page 36.

Anticipatory Set: Ask five students to line up at the front of the room, and without saying anything, put them in boy-girl order. Then ask the rest of the class to guess whether a boy or girl would go next in line. Have the students explain how they know. Then tell them that they have identified a pattern.

Purpose: Explain that the students are going to look at patterns, and using what they see, they will complete or extend the patterns.

Input: Define *pattern* as a sequence of repeating things.

Modeling: Place the pattern sheet, page 36, on the overhead. Show the students the first row. Ask the students to add two more items in the pattern. Ask the students to identify the pattern. Tell them that since it is alternating, it is an *A-B* pattern. Write the letters on the lines. Then, repeat for the next pattern. Explain that this is an *A-A-B* pattern. Repeat for the *AABB* and *ABB* patterns.

Guided Practice: Tell the students to choose a partner. Pass out page 37. Explain the directions. Tell the students that the partners will work on completing the pattern and identifying it as an *A-B* pattern. Monitor the students as they work.

Check for Understanding: Review the problems together. Have one set of partners identify the pattern and another complete the pattern.

Independent Practice: Pass out page 38. Explain that the students will now apply what they learned about patterns by making their own examples of patterns. They must draw pictures to fit a given pattern.

Closure: Review what patterns are. Then ask the students to identify real life situations that use patterns.

Name _____   Date _____

Patterns

Directions

Finish the pattern with two more shapes. Then, identify the pattern.

1.

_____

2.

_____

3.

_____

4.

_____

Unit 2: Math

Lesson Plans Using Graphic Organizers 2, SV 2070-2

Name _____   Date _____

Completing Patterns

Directions

Look at the patterns. Fill in the missing items. Write the name of the pattern in the blank.

_____ 1.

_____ 2.

_____ 3.

_____ 4.

_____ 5.

Unit 2: Math

Lesson Plans Using Graphic Organizers 2, SV 2070-2

Make the Pattern

Directions

Look at the pattern name. Draw pictures to go with that pattern.

1. ABAB:

2. ABB:

3. AAB:

4. AABB:

5. ABB:

6. AB:

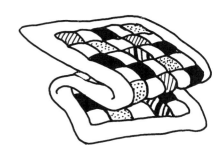

Tool 9 Skip-Counting

Preparation: Make copies of pages 41 and 42 for students. Make an overhead of page 40.

Anticipatory Set: Ask four students to line up at the front of the room. Have them hold their hands up, palms out and fingers open. Ask students what would be a quick and easy way to count all of the fingers. Then explain that counting by fives is skip-counting.

Purpose: Explain that the students are going to look at sets of numbers and count by skipping a given amount between each number.

Input: Define *skip-counting* as counting by leaving out numbers.

Modeling: Place the pattern sheet, page 40, on the overhead. Read the information at the top of the page. Show the students the first row. Ask a student to add two more shoes to four and tell how many shoes there are (6). Fill that number in the blank. Proceed by filling in the rest of the numbers. Then, point out that the person in the problem is counting by twos. Therefore, the students are skip-counting by twos.

Guided Practice: Tell the students to choose a partner. Pass out page 41. Explain the directions. Tell the students that the partners will skip-count by threes. They need to fill in the missing numbers.

Check for Understanding: Review the missing numbers together. Have one set of partners identify the missing numbers, and then have everyone count by threes from 3 to 60.

Independent Practice: Explain that the students will now apply what they learned about patterns by skip-counting by twos, threes, fives, and by odd numbers. They need to look for the pattern and fill in the missing numbers. Explain that some of the patterns are counting backwards.

Closure: Review what it means to skip-count. Then, ask students to identify examples of real world experiences in which they may use skip-counting.

Too Many Shoes!

Miss Smith has a shoe store. She has many pairs of shoes. She wants to know how many shoes she has in her store. She tries to count the shoes, but sometimes she loses her place. Help Miss Smith count the shoes by filling in the numbers she missed.

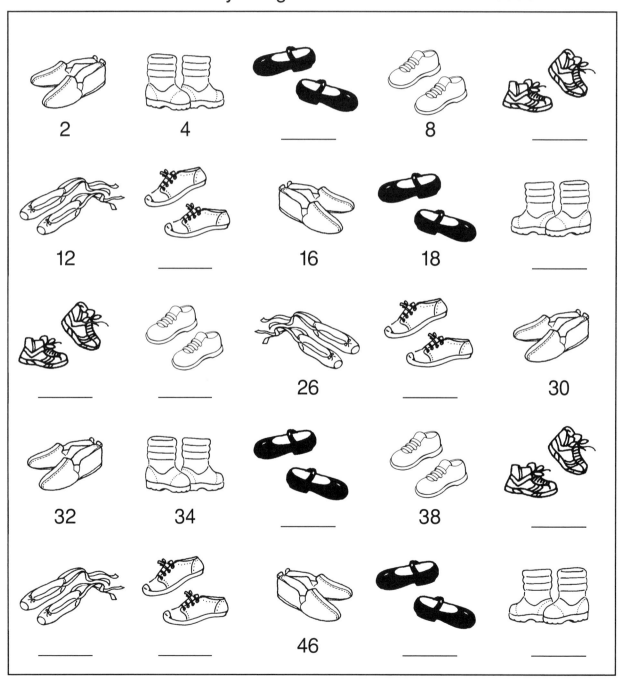

Name _____   Date _____

A Forest Full Of Threes

Sandy works in the forest. One day she decides to count all the trees. The trees in Sandy's forest all grow in groups of three. Help Sandy count the trees by filling in the missing numbers.

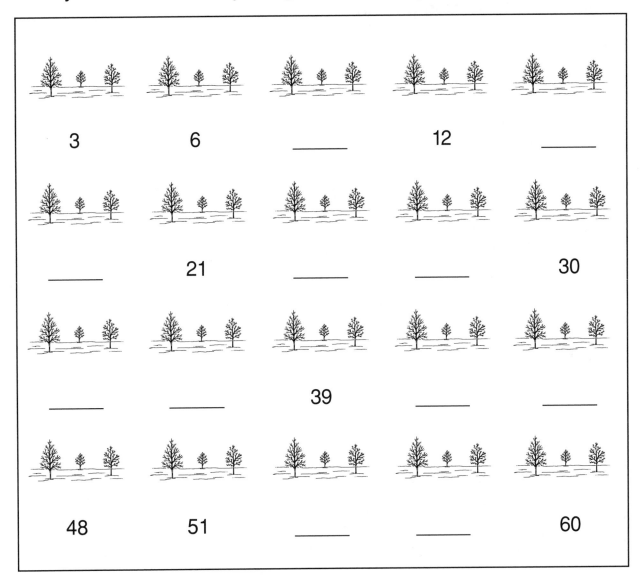

3   6   _____   12   _____

_____   21   _____   _____   30

_____   _____   39   _____   _____

48   51   _____   _____   60

Math Madness

Harriet loves balloons. One day she wrote numbers on a lot of balloons and let them go. But she forgot to write numbers on some balloons. Help Harriet. Find a pattern in each group of balloons. Then fill in the missing numbers.

1.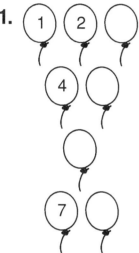

2.

3.

4.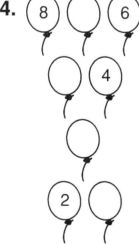

5.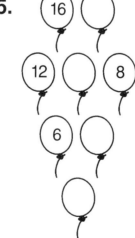

6.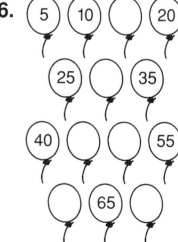

Tool 10 Using a Chart

Preparation: Copy pages 45 and 46 for students. Make an overhead of page 44.

Anticipatory Set: Show the picture of the chart on page 44. Ask the students to tell you what they know just by looking at the chart. Ask why they might need to use one of these.

Purpose: Discuss the purpose of charts. Explain that most charts are used to show information, or data, so the facts can easily be read or understood. Tell the students that they are going to use charts to help solve math problems.

Input: Explain that the chart has information. Check the title first and also check to see what kind of information is included in the chart.

Modeling: Return to the chart about tulips on the overhead. Read the information shown on the chart. Then read questions 1 and 2, and work the problems together. Explain your thinking process out loud to model for the students how you interpret the graph and to make sure the students understand how to read the graph.

Guided Practice: Divide the students into partners. Pass out page 45. Read the directions together, and talk through the process. Let the students complete the two problems with their partners. Monitor to check for progress.

Check for Understanding: Review the purpose of a chart. Check for those qualities in this chart. Then go over the answers to the two problems.

Independent Practice: Hand out page 46. Read the information together and explain the activity. Monitor the students as they work individually.

Closure: Have students review the purpose of a chart. Show the sample problem again on the overhead. Review how to read a chart. Ask for any examples of real world applications of a chart.

Tulip Days

Sometimes a problem has many facts. If you put the facts in a chart, you can see how the facts go together.

Directions

Read the problem.

Anne bought 1 white, 3 red, 9 yellow, and 5 purple tulips. Tom bought 2 white, 2 red, 7 yellow, and 10 purple tulips. Donna bought 8 white, 4 red, 1 yellow, and 6 purple tulips. Who bought more yellow tulips, Anne or Tom? How many more?

Make a chart.

Tulips Bought

	Anne	Tom	Donna
White tulips	1	2	8
Red tulips	3	2	4
Yellow tulips	9	7	1
Purple tulips	5	10	6

To solve the problem, read the chart.

Anne bought 9 yellow tulips. Tom bought 7 yellow tulips.

Then subtract to find the answer.

9−7 = 2   So, Anne bought 2 more yellow tulips than Tom bought.

Now it's your turn! Use the chart to answer the problems.

1. Who bought more purple tulips, Tom or Donna?

_____

How many more?

_____

2. Donna bought how many more white tulips than Anne?

_____

44

Name _____   Date _____

Practicing with Charts

Sometimes a problem has many facts. If you put the facts in a chart, you can see how the facts go together.

Directions

Read the problem.

Lynn bought 3 mints, 4 candy bars, 6 gum balls, and 2 jelly beans. Duy bought 5 mints, 5 candy bars, 1 gum ball, and 6 jelly beans. Bill bought 6 mints, 3 candy bars, 3 gum balls, and 5 jelly beans. Who bought more jelly beans, Lynn or Bill? How many more?

Make a chart.

Candy Bought

	Lynn	Duy	Bill
mints	3	5	6
candy bars	4	5	3
gum balls	6	1	3
jelly beans	2	6	5

To solve the problem, read the chart.

Lynn bought 2 jelly beans. Bill bought 5 jelly beans.

Then, subtract to find the answer.

5 − 2 = 3. So, Bill bought 3 more jelly beans than Lynn.

Now it's your turn! Use the chart to answer the problems.

1. Who bought more gum balls, Duy or Lynn?

_____

How many more?

_____

2. Duy bought how many more candy bars than Bill?

_____

Unit 2: Math   Lesson Plans Using Graphic Organizers 2, SV 2070-2

Using a Chart

Sometimes a problem has many facts. If you put the facts in a chart, you can see how the facts go together.

Directions

Read the problem. Make a chart. To solve the problem, read the chart.

Darius bought 5 red, 4 yellow, 6 green, and 7 blue marbles. Delyn bought 6 red, 2 yellow, 8 green, and 2 blue marbles. Brianna bought 6 red, 1 yellow, 10 green, and 4 blue marbles. Who bought more yellow marbles, Darius or Delyn? How many more?

Marbles Bought

	Darius	Delyn	Brianna
red			
yellow			
green			
blue			

Darius bought _____ yellow marbles. Delyn bought _____ yellow marbles.

Write an equation: _____ – _____ = _____

So, _____ has _____ more yellow marbles than _____.

Now it's your turn! Use the chart to answer the problems.

1. Who bought more green marbles, Darius or Brianna?

_____

2. How many more blue marbles did Brianna buy than Delyn?

_____

Tool 11   Using a Calendar

Preparation: Make copies of pages 49 and 50 for the students. Make overheads of pages 48 and 49. Have a wall calendar handy.

Anticipatory Set: Point to a calendar, and ask the students what a calendar is for. Then, point out that the days of the week are on top, and that the dates run sequentially from left to right.

Purpose: Tell the students that they are going to use a calendar to solve problems.

Input: Review the months of the year, days of the week, and how many days are in a week. Explain that a date consists of a day, month, and year.

Modeling: Place page 48 on the overhead. Compare the number of days in each month. Then review the months. Read the directions, and work through the eight questions. Then place page 49 on the overhead. Explain that the students are going to fill in a calendar for this month. They are going to write in the dates, the month's name, and the year. Tell the students how many days are in the month. Write in the first day. Then, write in the first week, showing how the numbers wrap at the end of the row to the next. Write in the last date. Put a list on the board of this month's holidays or special events with their dates. Write in one of the holidays or events.

Guided Practice: Divide the students into partners. Explain that with a partner the students are going to complete filling in the calendar. They will label the calendar with the month's name and the year. Then, they will fill in the holidays and special events. Leave your model and list on the overhead.

Check for Understanding: Focus the students on the overhead. Have several students tell how they filled in the calendar. Ask the students to tell where they put in the holidays and events. Then, have the students make any corrections to their calendars.

Independent Practice: Now, explain that the students will use their calendar to answer questions. Remind them that when the question asks for a date, the students need to write a month, day, and year (ex., January 23, 2000). Read through the questions, and discuss possible answers on the overhead calendar. Then, pass out page 50, and have the students answer the questions independently. After the students complete the questions, they can draw a picture that depicts features of the month on top of the calendar on page 49.

Closure: Review the parts of a calendar. Ask the students to think up questions to ask each other. For example, what is the date of the second Friday? Have them think of reasons why we need calendars.

Name _____ Date _____

All Year Long

Directions

Circle these dates on the calendar.

1. the first day of June
2. the last day of September
3. Thanksgiving Day, November 26
4. Independence Day, July 4
5. Valentine's Day, February 14
6. Mother's Day, May 10
7. Father's Day, June 21

Calendar

	January							February							March							April					
S	M	T	W	T	F	S	S	M	T	W	T	F	S	S	M	T	W	T	F	S	S	M	T	W	T	F	S
			1	2	3	4							1	1	2	3	4	5	6	7					1	2	3	4
5	6	7	8	9	10	11	2	3	4	5	6	7	8	8	9	10	11	12	13	14	5	6	7	8	9	10	11
12	13	14	15	16	17	18	9	10	11	12	13	14	15	15	16	17	18	19	20	21	12	13	14	15	16	17	18
19	20	21	22	23	24	25	16	17	18	19	20	21	22	22	23	24	25	26	27	28	19	20	21	22	23	24	25
26	27	28	29	30	31		23	24	25	26	37	28	29	29	30	31					26	27	28	29	30		

	May							June							July							August					
S	M	T	W	T	F	S	S	M	T	W	T	F	S	S	M	T	W	T	F	S	S	M	T	W	T	F	S
					1	2	1	2	3	4	5	6					1	2	3	4							1
3	4	5	6	7	8	9	7	8	9	10	11	12	13	5	6	7	8	9	10	11	2	3	4	5	6	7	8
10	11	12	13	14	15	16	14	15	16	17	18	19	20	12	13	14	15	16	17	18	9	10	11	12	13	14	15
17	18	19	20	21	22	23	21	22	23	24	25	26	27	19	20	21	22	23	24	25	16	17	18	19	20	21	22
24/31	25	26	27	28	29	30	28	29	30					26	27	28	29	30	31		23/30	24/31	25	26	27	28	29

	September							October							November							December					
S	M	T	W	T	F	S	S	M	T	W	T	F	S	S	M	T	W	T	F	S	S	M	T	W	T	F	S
		1	2	3	4	5					1	2	3	1	2	3	4	5	6	7			1	2	3	4	5
6	7	8	9	10	11	12	4	5	6	7	8	9	10	8	9	10	11	12	13	14	6	7	8	9	10	11	12
13	14	15	16	17	18	19	11	12	13	14	15	16	17	15	16	17	18	19	20	21	13	14	15	16	17	18	19
20	21	22	23	24	25	26	18	19	20	21	22	23	24	22	23	24	25	26	27	28	20	21	22	23	24	25	26
27	28	29	30				25	26	27	28	29	30	31	29	30						27	28	29	30	31		

Solve.

8. Paula's birthday is 7 days before Peter's birthday. Paula's birthday is on Friday. On what day is Peter's birthday?

_____

Name _____ Date _____

Calendar

Sunday	Monday	Tuesday	Wednesday	Thursday	Friday	Saturday

Unit 2: Math

Lesson Plans Using Graphic Organizers 2, SV 2070-2

Calendar Questions

Directions

Complete the calendar. Use the information on the calendar to answer the questions.

1. What is today's date? _____

2. What is the date of the third Sunday? _____

3. On what day of the week did this month begin? _____

4. On what day of the week will this month end? _____

5. On what day of the week will next month begin? _____

6. What holidays are in this month? _____

What are their dates? _____

7. How many days will we go to school this month? _____

8. How many Mondays are in this month? _____

9. Find the 15th. What is the date 7 days after the 15th? _____

10. What is the date of the first Friday? _____

Bonus: Write your own calendar question and its answer.

_____

_____

_____

_____

Tool 12 Identifying Solid Figures

Preparation: Make copies of pages 53 and 54 for students. Make overheads of pages 52 and 53.

Anticipatory Set: Show the top row of solids on page 52 on the overhead. Review their names and discuss the shapes. Then ask several students to find examples of each solid in the classroom (ex., tissue box for the rectangular prism).

Purpose: Explain that these are solid shapes. Tell the students that they are going to identify these shapes and match them with similar shapes.

Input: Identify the five solid shapes: sphere, cone, cylinder, cube, and rectangular prism.

Modeling: Review the five shapes. Cover the words, and have different students identify them by name. Then, uncover the first row by problem number one. Ask the students to identify the shape on the left side. Then, have them identify the four on the right. Ask the students to tell which shape on the right matches the one on the left. Repeat this for the five rows.

Guided Practice: Divide the students in partners. Place page 53 on the overhead. Review the shapes and their names. Pass out page 53, and read the directions. Have the students complete the page with their partners.

Check for Understanding: Review the five shapes. Ask students to tell which shapes matched in each row. As they tell you an answer, circle it on the overhead of that page. Have them make corrections as you write on the overhead.

Independent Practice: Explain that the students will need to use the information they have on solid shapes to identify them in pictures. Pass out page 54. Read the directions. Introduce the new shape, the pyramid. Explain that they will need crayons to complete this assignment. Remind them to identify the shapes in each picture carefully.

Closure: Review the six solid shapes. Have the students give examples of real-world things that have each shape. Have them make collections of pictures of shapes or things to reinforce their understanding of shapes.

Copy:
pg 55 - (1)
56, 57 (2)

Identifying Solids

  sphere

cone

cylinder

cube

rectangular prism

Directions

Ring the matching shape.

1. |

2.

3.

4.

5.

Unit 2: Math

Name _____   Date _____

Matching Solids

spheres   cones   cylinders   cubes   rectangular prisms

Directions

Ring the matching shape.

1.

2.

3.

4. Match

Unit 2: Math
Lesson Plans Using Graphic Organizers 2, SV 2070-2

Searching for Solids

1. Color each ⬭ red.   Color each ⬭ purple.

Color each ⬜ green.   Color each ▯ brown.

Color each △ blue.   Color each △ orange.

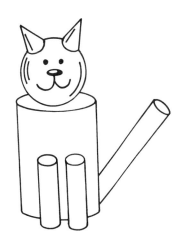

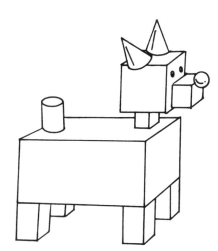

2. Count each shape. Write how many.

54

Tool 13 Estimating Measurement

Preparation: Make copies of pages 57 and 58 for students. Make an overhead of page 56.

Anticipatory Set: Ask two students of different height to stand in front of the class. Ask both of them to guess how many feet tall they are. Show them a foot ruler. Write their estimations on the board. Measure each student, and write the actual height on the board. Tell the students that the first measurement was an estimation and the second was actual.

Purpose: Tell the students that they are going to estimate measurements, then find the actual length.

Input: Explain that *estimating* means to make a good guess.

Modeling: Put page 56 on the overhead. Show the paintbrushes to the students. Cover all of the brushes but number one. Ask a student to estimate, or guess, how many paper clips long the brush is. Write the guess in the blank. Take a paper clip and measure how many paper clips long the brush is. Write in the approximate number in the space. Ask the students how close they were with their estimation. Repeat for the next three problems.

Guided Practice: Explain that now the students are going to use a ruler to help them estimate the length of objects around the room. Show them the ruler. Point to the twelve inches. Divide the students into partners. Pass out one ruler per set of partners. Have them touch each inch as you count them. Show them how to start measuring at zero and going up. Pass out page 57. Practice measuring the bottom of the page. Then read the directions. Explain that they will estimate the length first, then they will measure the item with the ruler. Have the students work with their partners.

Check for Understanding: Review what it means to estimate. Have different sets of partners tell their estimation and the actual length of each item.

Independent Practice: Explain that the students will now use the rulers to measure and predict the length of ribbon on page 58. Pass out the page and a ruler to those who do not have one. Read the directions, and explain that for each problem they are to draw two lines: the estimated and the actual.

Closure: Review what *estimation* means. Ask the students to describe situations that they would have to use estimation.

Brushing Up on Measuring

Directions

Use a small paper clip to measure each brush. Write the length.

1.

guess _____   about _____ clips

2.

guess _____   about _____ clips

3.

guess _____   about _____ clips

4.

guess _____   about _____ clips

Unit 2: Math

Estimating Lengths

Directions

Estimate the length of the object. Then measure it with a ruler. Write down the length.

1. What is the length of your math book?

My guess: _____ inches   Actual: _____ inches

2. What is the length of your desk?

My guess: _____ inches   Actual: _____ inches

3. What is the length of the bookshelf?

My guess: _____ inches   Actual: _____ inches

4. What is the length of the door?

My guess: _____ inches   Actual: _____ inches

5. What is the length of your pencil?

My guess: _____ inches   Actual: _____ inches

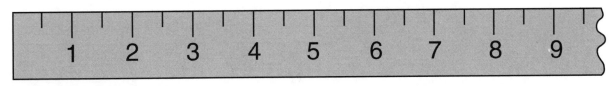

inches

Name _____   Date _____

Inching Along

Directions

Draw a line that is your estimate. Then use an inch ruler to draw the actual pieces of ribbon.

1. 2 inches

2. 5 inches

3. 3 inches

Solve.

4. Rhonda needs 4 inches of ribbon.
Draw a line to show where she will cut.

Tool 14 Making Fractions

Preparation: Make copies of pages 61 and 62 for students. Make an overhead of page 60.

Anticipatory Set: Ask four students to line up at the front of the room, three girls and one boy. Ask the class how many students are standing. Write *4* on the board. Then draw a line above it. Then ask how many of them are girls. Then write *3* above the *4* on the board. Explain that this is a fraction; three of the four students are girls.

Purpose: Explain that the students are going to look at pictures and write fractions based on the pictures.

Input: Explain the parts of a fraction. Define *numerator* and *denominator* as parts in relation to the whole.

Modeling: Place page 60 on the overhead. Read the information about fractions. Go through each step and discuss each process. Then, work the problems together.

Guided Practice: Tell the students to choose a partner. Pass out page 61. Read the directions, and have a student restate the directions. Let the students work the problems together.

Check for Understanding: Review the parts of the fraction, the numerator and denominator. Reread the problems, and ask for volunteers to give the answers.

Independent Practice: Explain that the students will now apply what they know about fractions on another sheet. Pass out page 62. Read the directions, and make sure each student has crayons. Work the first problem together, and then have the students do the rest independently.

Closure: Review how to set up a fraction. Review that the bottom number, or denominator, is the total number, and the top number, or numerator, is the part. Ask the students if they can think of anything that they eat or use that can be a fraction (ex. pizza, pie, candy bar, etc.).

Parts of a Whole

A fraction names equal parts of a whole, or equal parts of a group. Each fraction has two numbers. The top number is called the numerator. The bottom number is called the denominator.

$$\text{numerator} \longrightarrow \frac{1}{2} \longleftarrow \text{denominator}$$

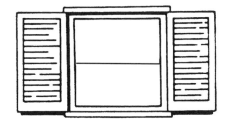

Directions

Read the problem.

Bill is helping around the house. Today he is washing this window. The window has 2 equal parts. Bill is supposed to wash 1 of the parts, or one half. Shade in the part of the window that Bill will wash.

Identify the facts.

Fact 1:   The window has 2 equal parts.

Fact 2:   Bill is supposed to wash 1 part.

Decide what the problem is asking.

Shade in $\frac{1}{2}$, or one half, of the window.

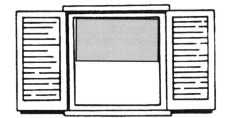

Solve the problem.

Shade in 1 part.

Now, shade in 1 part on Window B and Window C.

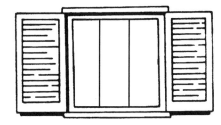

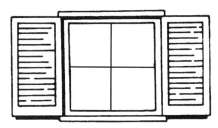

Window B has 3 equal parts.   Window C has 4 equal parts.
Each part is $\frac{1}{3}$, or one third.   Each part is $\frac{1}{4}$, or one fourth.

60   Lesson Plans Using Graphic Organizers 2, SV 2070-2

Unit 2: Math

Name _____   Date _____

Fractured Fractions

Sometimes a drawing helps you to understand a problem.

Directions

Now it's your turn! Study the drawings below to solve the problems.

1. This window has 4 equal parts. Bill is supposed to wash 1 of the parts, or one fourth. Shade in $\frac{1}{4}$ of the window.

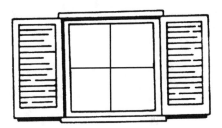

2. This window has 3 equal parts. Bill must wash 2 of the parts, or two thirds. The fraction is $\frac{2}{3}$. Shade $\frac{2}{3}$ of the window.

3. This window has 5 equal parts. Bill must wash 3 of the parts, or three fifths. The fraction is $\frac{3}{5}$. Shade in $\frac{3}{5}$ of the window.

4. This window has 6 equal parts. Bill breaks one of the parts, or one sixth. The fraction is $\frac{1}{6}$. Shade in $\frac{1}{6}$ of the window that Bill has broken.

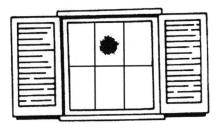

Unit 2: Math

© Steck-Vaughn Company   Lesson Plans Using Graphic Organizers 2, SV 2070-2

Name _____   Date _____

Baking Up Fractions

Color to show the fractions.

1.

$\frac{1}{3}$ green, $\frac{2}{3}$ yellow

2.

$\frac{2}{3}$ orange, $\frac{1}{3}$ red

3.

$\frac{2}{5}$ blue, $\frac{3}{5}$ orange

4.

$\frac{4}{5}$ purple, $\frac{1}{5}$ yellow

5.

$\frac{3}{4}$ green, $\frac{1}{4}$ purple

6.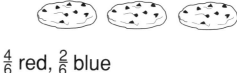

$\frac{4}{6}$ red, $\frac{2}{6}$ blue

Solve.

7. Mr. Ruiz uses $\frac{2}{6}$ of his eggs to make cookies. Color the number of eggs Mr. Ruiz uses.

Tool 15   Changing Matter

Preparation: Make copies of pages 65 and 66 for students. Make an overhead of page 64. Gather a balloon, clear glass of water, and a pencil.

Anticipatory Set: Show the students the three objects. Blow up the balloon, and ask them what is inside the balloon. Explain that there is air inside, which is a gas. Ask the students to describe the water. After they mention several attributes, tell them it is a liquid. Finally, have them describe the pencil, and tell them it is a solid.

Purpose: Explain that the students are going to sort things as solid, liquid, or gas, and they are going to identify what characteristics those three states of matter possess.

Input: Define the three states of matter, using water as a model. Have the students refer to ice for solid, water for liquid, and vapor for gas.

Modeling: Place page 64 on the overhead. Read the information about water. Discuss other things that are solids, liquids, and gases. Then, match the words with the state of matter.

Guided Practice: Divide the students into partners. Pass out page 65. Read the directions to the students. Then, read the riddles. Have the students answer the riddles with their partner.

Check for Understanding: Reread each riddle, calling on students to give answers. Then, review the three states of matter. Have the students brainstorm other examples of solids, liquids, and gases.

Independent Practice: Pass out page 66. Read the directions. Have the students work independently to identify each item as a solid, liquid, or gas.

Closure: Review the three states of matter. Ask the students to remember ice, water, and vapor to identify states of matter. Have them think of other examples of liquids they use daily, of solids that they own, and gases that they have used. Make a poster with all of their suggestions labeled under three categories: *solid*, *liquid*, *gas*.

Wonderful Water

Water is an interesting kind of matter. It can be a solid, a liquid, or a gas. If water is a solid, it is ice. We can drink liquid water or use it in other ways. Water that is a gas is called water vapor.

Water can change from one form to another. If you freeze liquid water, it becomes a solid. If you melt the solid ice, it becomes a liquid. If you leave a glass of liquid water out without covering it, it evaporates and becomes a gas. This gas is invisible and is part of the air.

(Directions)

Draw lines to match the words on the left with the words on the right.

1. ice   liquid

2. water vapor   solid

3. water   gas

Name _____   Date _____

What Am I?

Use one of these words to answer each question.
Write the word on the line.

| matter   solid   liquid   gas |

1. I can be soft or hard. I can be big or small. I have a shape.
What am I?

_____

2. I can pour. My shape can change. I am wet. What am I?

_____

3. You cannot see me. I have no shape. You can feel me when I
am wind. What am I?

_____

4. I am what things are made of. I have three forms. What am I?

_____

Solids, Liquids, and Gases

Matter can be a solid, a liquid, or a gas. You can see a solid. It holds its shape. You can see a liquid. It takes the shape of the container. You cannot see a gas. However, it takes the shape of the container also.

Directions

Write S under solids, L under liquids, and G under gases.

1. _____

2. _____

3. _____

4. _____

5. _____

6. _____

7. _____

8. _____

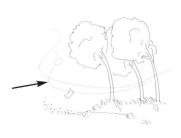

9. _____

Tool 16 Observing Weather

Preparation: Make copies of pages 69 and 70 for students. Make an overhead of page 68. Get a newspaper for five days in a row, or arrange to watch the weather channel every day at the same time.

Anticipatory Set: Ask the students to brainstorm the different types of weather they have seen in the last month. Write their answers on the board.

Purpose: Explain that the students are going to observe the weather for a few days and make predictions about the weather.

Input: Explain that weather is a combination of wind, precipitation, and air pressure.

Modeling: Explain that the students are going to observe and record the weather. Put page 68 on the overhead. Show the students how to make a prediction and then how to record the actual weather. Do the first day together. (Have the students do their sheet with their partners from the Guided Practice after you do yours. Let them use the newspaper or television.) Repeat every day for the week.

Guided Practice: Divide the students into groups. Pass out page 69. Read the directions to the students. Then, explain that they will use the newspaper or television to record the weather information.

Check for Understanding: Discuss what the students observed from the newspaper or television. Then, observe the difference between the days' temperature, weather, and wind. Ask how accurate their predictions were.

Independent Practice: On the final day, ask the students to review their observations of the weather. Pass out page 70. Have the students answer the questions independently.

Closure: Review the different types of weather. Tell the students to observe the weather. Ask them to think of reasons why it is good to know what the weather will be.

What Will the Weather Be?

Directions

Fill in the chart, and answer the questions.

	Monday	Tuesday	Wednesday	Thursday	Friday
We Think					
What the Weather Is					

What do you see?

1. Did the weather change?

_____

2. Did you make good guesses?

_____

What do you think?

3. Tell how you know what guesses to make.

_____

68

Name _____ Date _____

Predicting the Weather

Get weather information from the newspaper, radio, and TV. Use any weather instruments you have. Use your senses, too. Then, fill in the weather log and predict the next day's weather.

	Sunny	Partly Cloudy	Cloudy	Rain	Snow	Wind — Not Windy	Wind — Slightly Windy	Wind — Very Windy	Temperature	Prediction for Tomorrow
SUNDAY Date ____										
MONDAY Date ____										
TUESDAY Date ____										
WEDNESDAY Date ____										
THURSDAY Date ____										
FRIDAY Date ____										
SATURDAY Date ____										

Unit 3: Science

Lesson Plans Using Graphic Organizers 2, SV 2070-2

Language of Science

Directions

Use these words to fill in the blanks.

Sun	Fog	wind	water vapor
longer	temperature	clouds	

1. A thermometer measures _____.

2. Moving air is called _____.

3. The _____ warms the air during the day.

4. Rain and snow fall from _____.

5. The line inside the thermometer gets _____ as the temperature gets hotter.

6. _____ is a low cloud near the ground.

7. When water goes into the air, it is called _____

_____.

(Tool 17) Finding Fossils

Preparation: Make copies of pages 73 and 74 for the students. Make an overhead of page 72. Gather samples of fossils of plants and animals. Also bring a bag of store-bought chocolate chip cookies and ice cream sticks.

Anticipatory Set: On the board, have students brainstorm a list of things they know about fossils. Have the students tell where they came from, what they are, what they look like, and where they can be found.

Purpose: Tell the students that they are going to learn about paleontologists and fossils.

Input: Define a *fossil* as a print or hardened shape of a plant or an animal. A *paleontologist* is someone who studies fossils.

Modeling: Pass around several samples of fossils. Have the students observe things about the fossils. Then, place page 72 on the overhead. Read the information about fossils, and have the students discuss how the rock layers formed. Then, read the directions. Have several students suggest what types of fossils to draw in the bottom layer.

Guided Practice: Explain that scientists use the layers of rocks to identify fossils. Pass out page 73. Read the information out loud to the students. Discuss the different fossils in each layer. Read the directions, and have the students color the fossils and answer the question.

Check for Understanding: Review what fossils are and how scientists know when a certain animal or plant lived based on its fossil's location. Ask the students to tell which fossils they colored. Ask several students to tell how they know that the fossil is the oldest.

Independent Practice: Tell the students that they are going to become paleontologists. Pass out page 74. Read the information about paleontologists and what they do. Read the directions. Have the students work on the paper while you pass out a chocolate chip cookie and an ice cream stick to each student. After they finish their sheet, have the students use the ice cream sticks to dig for chips. Tell them to pretend that they are paleontologists and that they are digging for the chocolate-chip fossils. They have to break apart the cookie and extract the chips. Have them chart their chips from the cookie on the back of their paper.

Closure: Review how fossils are made and what paleontologists do. Ask the students to discuss why it is important for scientists to chart on grids where they found the fossils, and why it is important to learn about fossils.

Layers of Rock

A **fossil** is the print or hardened shape of a plant or an animal. Fossils are found in rock layers. These layers of rock were once soil. Plants and animals that died became buried in the soil. Over many years, because of the pressure of all the soil above it, the soil became rock. New layers of rock keep forming over older layers.

Directions

Draw and color some fossils in the oldest rock layer in the picture.

Fascinating Fossils

Since different rock layers form at different times, the fossils found in the layers are different, too. This helps scientists know when certain plants and animals lived. For example, fossils of starfish were found in deeper layers of rock than fossils of dinosaurs. Which animal lived first?

(Directions)

**Color the oldest fossils in the picture.
How do you know they are the oldest?**

_____

_____

Digging In

Scientists who are interested in knowing about plants and animals that lived long ago are called **paleontologists**. One way paleontologists find out about the past is by finding and observing fossils.

Paleontologists must be very careful when they dig for fossils. They must not break the fossils they find. They often make a map to show exactly where they find the fossils.

Directions

Imagine that you are the paleontologist who found this fossil. Use the grid to draw where you found it.

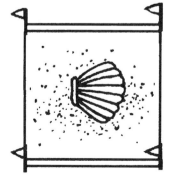
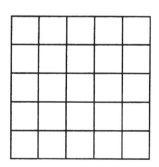

Tool 18   Making Shadows

Preparation: Make copies of pages 77 and 78 for the students. Make an overhead of page 76. Have a piece of chalk and a ruler for each student.

Anticipatory Set: Turn off all of the lights and turn on the overhead. Put your hand up and cast a shadow onto the wall. Ask the students if the shadow looks like your hand or if it is different. Ask what causes the shadow. Ask what other things cause shadows.

Purpose: Explain that the students are going to study how the Sun makes shadows.

Input: Define *shadow* as the result of when something blocks the light.

Modeling: Place page 76 on the overhead. Read the information about shadows. Then, look at the pictures. Ask the students to look closely at the pictures and identify which shadows match their pictures. Talk about how the shadows have to look like the objects casting them.

Guided Practice: Pass out page 77. Tell the students that they are going to make some observations about their own shadow. Take the students outside and line them up on the sidewalk. Ask them to look at their shadows. Explain that they are going to do this three times today. Each time, they are going to work with a partner to record what they observe about their shadows. Have one student per partner team draw an *X* with the chalk on the ground where he or she is standing and write his or her name beside it. Have the other partner trace the shadow with the chalk. Use a ruler to measure how long the shadow is. Have the students observe in which direction the shadows are being cast. Have them do the same for their partners. Repeat this process, having the students use the same *X* two more times.

Check for Understanding: After each trip outside, have the partners return to the classroom and complete the chart on page 77. Then, have the students discuss their observations. After the last trip outside, have the students answer the questions. Discuss their answers. Ask them to discuss what caused their shadows to change. Discuss how their shadows changed when the Sun moved.

Independent Practice: Have the students take a final trip back out to their *X*'s. Have them bring their crayons and pencils and something hard to write on. Then, pass out page 78. Read the information to the students. Have the students draw in their changing shadows. Remind them that their shadow moved as the Sun moved.

Closure: Review the relationship between the Sun and shadows. Tell students to observe their shadows in the evening and in the morning. Ask them how their shadows might change on a rainy day.

Shapes of Shadows

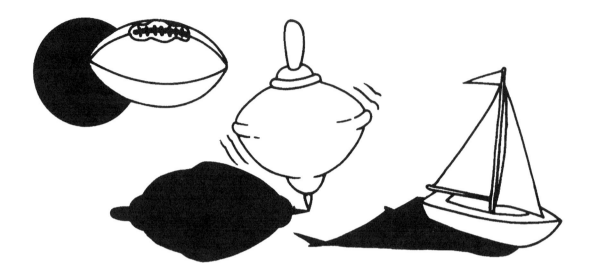

Look at shadows around you. Is the shadow of a pencil the same shape as the pencil? Is the shadow of a bicycle the same shape as a bicycle? You will see that shadows have a shape that is like the object that makes them. Why do you think this is so?

When an object blocks light, the rays of light are stopped by the object. Other light rays go past the object's edges. The shadow is the area that the light rays cannot get to.

Directions

In the pictures above, color the toys that have the correct shadows.

Measuring Your Shadow

Directions

Go out on a sunny day. Make an <u>X</u> on the blacktop. Stand on the <u>X</u>. Have a friend trace your shadow. Measure your shadow. Do this three different times. Fill in the chart.

Materials:
chalk
a ruler

Time	How long is your shadow?	Show which way your shadow goes.
10:00	_____ inches	
12:00	_____ inches	
2:00	_____ inches	

1. What happens to your shadow?

_____

_____

2. Can you see your shadow on a cloudy day?

_____

Outdoor Shadows

If you went outdoors and measured the same shadow at two different times, you would find that the shadow changes size. Why does this happen?

The size and position of a shadow change because the position of the Sun changes. Look at where the Sun is in these pictures. Look at the size and position of the shadow.

You can see that the size and position of the shadow changed as the position of the Sun changed.

Directions

In these three boxes, draw your own changing shadows.

1.	2.	3.

Unit 3: Science

Tool 19 Sorting Rocks

Preparation: Make copies of pages 81 and 82 for the students. Make an overhead of page 80. Gather a large collection of rocks. Put twenty into a container, and have enough containers full of rocks for groups of three students.

Anticipatory Set: Write the word *rocks* on the board. Have the students tell you as much information as they can about rocks. Ask them to think about what rocks are, where they can be found, what they can be used for, and what they look like.

Purpose: Explain that the students are going to make observations about rocks and how they are used.

Input: Explain that there are several types of rocks, including granite, limestone, and pumice.

Modeling: Place page 80 on the overhead. Read the information about rocks. Then, fill in the sentences using the information. Discuss the three different types of rocks.

Guided Practice: Divide the students into groups of three. Pass out page 81. Tell the students that they are going to sort a collection of rocks. They must decide among themselves how to sort them. After they sort the rocks, they must complete the activity page.

Check for Understanding: Have the students stay in their groups. Ask each group individually to tell how they sorted their rocks and why they chose to sort them that way. Review the different types of rocks, and ask the students to identify at least one sample of each in their collections.

Independent Practice: Tell the students that they are now going to observe how rocks are used and how they change. Ask students if they have ever seen a crack in the sidewalk. Talk about what might have caused the sidewalk to crack. Pass out page 82, and read the directions. Have the students get a pencil and something on which to write. Take the students on a walk around the entire school. Have them make observations about the different uses of rocks, how they change, and what causes the change. After the walk, have several students share their observations with the rest of the class.

Closure: Review the three types of rocks. Review how rocks are used and how they change.

Name _____   Date _____

Kinds of Rocks

Directions

Read the article.
Complete the sentences below.

There are many kinds of rocks. Granite is a hard rock used to make buildings. Some rocks, like limestone, can be soft. Limestone was formed by dead ocean plants and animals. Pumice is a very light rock. Some pumice rocks can even float in water!

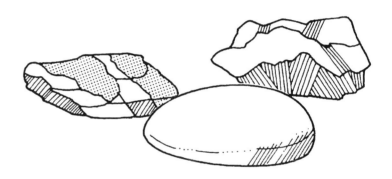

1. A rock used to make buildings is _____.

2. A rock that was formed by dead ocean plants and animals is

_____.

3. A rock that can float in water is _____.

Grouping Rocks

Directions

Sort the collection of rocks into groups. Draw a picture of a rock from each group. Then, write a sentence describing why you sorted that group the way you did.

1. Group one

2. Group two

3. Group three

4. Group four

Rocks Change

You are learning about how rocks are changed by wind, water, and plants. In this activity, you will observe how rocks are used and changed in your home and in your neighborhood.

A. In your home and neighborhood, look for rocks and for things made from rocks that are used by people.

B. Make the following observations about each thing:
   1. What kind of material is it?
   2. How is it used?
   3. If it is changing, explain how and why.

Directions

Fill in the chart below

Material	How It Is Used	How It Is Changing	Cause(s) of Change
Example: cement	sidewalk	cracks	weeds and/or grass

Tool 20   Creating a Birthday Graph

Preparation: Make copies of pages 85 and 86 for students. Make overheads of pages 84 and 85.

Anticipatory Set: Have the students list the months of the year. Block the months into seasons: December–February is winter, March–May is spring, June–August is summer, and September–November is fall. Ask the students to stand if their birthday is in the spring, then winter, then summer, and finally fall.

Purpose: Tell the students that they are going to graph their birthdays.

Input: Tell the students that they are going to use their birthday's month to make a graph.

Modeling: Tell the students that you are going to say a month, and the students who have a birthday in that month will raise their hands. Place page 84 on the overhead. As you say a month, write down the names of the students who have a birthday in that month. After you have tallied all twelve months, tell the students that they are now going to use this information to make a graph.

Guided Practice: Divide the students into partners. Pass out page 85. Have the students use crayons to color in the number of boxes per month for the number of people who have birthdays in that month. Point out the numbers running up the side, and the months along the bottom. Have the students create the graph using the information about the birthdays on the overhead.

Check for Understanding: Ask the students to tell you how many birthdays are in each month. As they tell you, fill in the graph on page 85 on the overhead. Have the students make corrections if they need to.

Independent Practice: Pass out page 86. Explain that the students are now going to answer questions using the information on their graph. Read the directions, and then read the questions out loud.

Closure: Review the purpose of graphing. Ask the students what else they can graph.

Name ______________________ Date ____________

Month by Month

Directions

Look at the birth dates on the board. Sort the birth dates into the correct month. Then put them in order from first to last in each month.

January

____
____
____

February

____
____
____

March

____
____
____

April

____
____
____

May

____
____
____

June

____
____
____

July

____
____
____

August

____
____
____

September

____
____
____

October

____
____
____

November

____
____
____

December

____
____
____

Birthday Graph

Directions

Use the information on the overhead to complete the graph.

	Jan.	Feb.	March	April	May	June	July	Aug.	Sept.	Oct.	Nov.	Dec.
11												
10												
9												
8												
7												
6												
5												
4												
3												
2												
1												

Name _____ Date _____

Counting Birthdays

Directions

Use the graph of birthdays to answer these questions.

1. How many students have birthdays in September?
   _____ students

2. How many students have birthdays in October?
   _____ students

3. Which month has the most birthdays? _____

4. Which month has the fewest birthdays? _____

5. Which month, June or July, has the most birthdays? _____
   How many more? _____

6. How many birthdays are in May and April?_____ birthdays

7. How many birthdays are there in all?_____ birthdays

8. How many summer birthdays are there? _____ birthdays

9. How many winter birthdays are there? _____ birthdays

10. Which season, winter, spring, summer, or fall, has the most
    birthdays?_____ How many? _____ birthdays

Unit 4: Social Studies
Lesson Plans Using Graphic Organizers 2, SV 2070-2

Tool 21 Knowing Your Community

Preparation: Copy pages 89 and 90 for students. Make overheads of pages 88 and 89.

Anticipatory Set: Ask the students to define *community*. Listen to their definitions.

Purpose: Tell the students that they are going to analyze the people, buildings, businesses, and important places in their community.

Input: Define *community* as the people and places in the neighborhood.

Modeling: Place page 88 on the overhead. Read the passage out loud. As you read have the students actively participate by answering the questions. Discuss the different places and people in their community.

Guided Practice: After reading, place page 89 on the overhead. In the middle, write *community*. Then, in the larger circles, write *people*, *buildings*, *businesses*, and *restaurants*. Tell the students to find a partner. Pass out page 89, and have the students write in the words you wrote on the overhead. Explain that the partners will work together to fill in examples of those categories. They will think up at least three examples for each category.

Check for Understanding: Have the students share their examples with the class. Write in some of their answers on the overhead sheet. Discuss how all of these pieces make up the community.

Independent Practice: Tell the students that they are going to think about their community and complete an activity sheet about themselves. They will fill in information about where they live, where they go to school, their favorite restaurant in their neighborhood, their favorite store, and how they get to school. They will draw pictures and write complete sentences.

Closure: Have several students share their information for each topic. Discuss the different types of places to live that exist in a community, the variety of stores and restaurants, and the different ways the students get to school. Ask how their community would be different if they lived somewhere else.

Home Zone

Whether you live in the country or in the city, the area around you is your neighborhood. What is in your neighborhood?

What do you see when you look out your windows at home? Do you see tall buildings and busy streets? Do you see trees and grass? Is your home in a big city? Or is it out in the country?

Whether you live in a city or in a town, you live in a neighborhood. Your neighborhood is the area around your home. If you live in an apartment building, you have many neighbors. If you live in a house, your neighbors live in the nearest houses.

What can you tell about your neighborhood? What is the name of your street? Are there stores and offices near you? Do you walk to school? Or do you take a bus to a school in another neighborhood? Is there a park or playground nearby?

Some neighborhoods are like a small city. Everything people need is there. In a city neighborhood, families can walk to restaurants. They walk to the post office and the library. Some neighborhoods have only houses. In these neighborhoods, stores and restaurants are farther away. People may drive to get where they need to go.

What can you learn about your neighborhood? What would a map of it look like? What streets and places would be on the map?

Using a Web

Topic:

Unit 4: Social Studies

My Community

Directions

Fill in the information about yourself.

1. Where I live:	**2.** Where I go to school:
3. How I get to school:	**4.** A building in my community:
5. A restaurant in my community:	**6.** A store in my community:

90

Tool 22 Mapping Skills

Preparation: Make copies of pages 93 and 94 for students. Make an overhead of page 92.

Anticipatory Set: Ask for a student to give you directions to get from your desk to the door. Follow the directions exactly to make a point. Then, ask another student to tell you how to get to the office. Next, ask a student to tell you how to get to another city. Ask the students what they might need to use if they don't know how to get somewhere.

Purpose: Explain that the students are going to learn how to read a map and use it to give directions. After they understand how to read a map, they will make a map of their own.

Input: Define the important things they will need to know, such as map key and compass rose. Explain that a *map key* tells what the symbols on a map represent. The *compass rose* gives directions—north, south, east, and west.

Modeling: Place page 92 on the overhead. Point to the compass rose. Review that the compass rose tells the directions, *N, S, E,* and *W.* Look at the map key. Go over what each symbol stands for, and locate it on the map. Ask a student to tell which direction someone would need to go from the castle to the third farm. Point to the castle and the third farm. Ask the student to tell you which direction to go (south). Then ask which direction someone would go from the first farm to the second. Ask for several other directions until you feel the students understand giving directions.

Guided Practice: Divide the students into partners. Pass out the map of the neighborhood on page 93. Have the students point to the map. Have the students point to the map key and then to the compass rose. Tell them to work with their partners to find the directions on the map. Read the questions, and then have them work with their partners.

Check for Understanding: Review the purpose of the map key and the compass rose. Review what each symbol represents. Read the questions, and have different students volunteer the answers.

Independent Practice: Tell the students that now that they have seen two types of maps, it is their turn to make a map. Tell them to make a map of the classroom. They need to make a map key, draw in a compass rose (tell them which way is north), and then draw the symbols in the map for everything in the classroom. Invite them to be creative with their symbols on the map but to be accurate.

Closure: Review the important elements of maps, including the map key and compass rose. Review the directions, north, south, east, and west. Then, have several students volunteer to share their maps of the classroom.

Using Map Keys

Directions

Look at the map key and the compass rose.

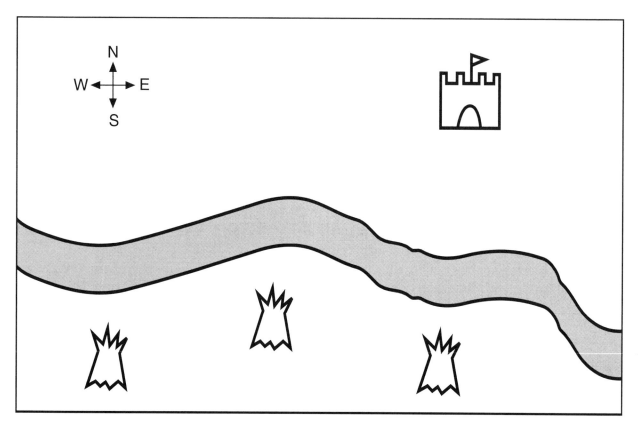

92

Name _____   Date _____

Stating Directions

Directions

Use the map, map key, and compass rose to answer the questions.

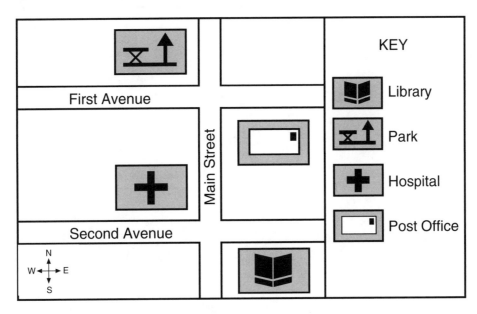

1. Which direction would you travel on Main Street to get from the library to the post office? _____

2. Draw the symbol for the park. _____

3. Which direction would you travel to go from the library to the hospital? _____

4. Which direction would you travel on First Avenue to go from the park to the post office? _____

5. What are the four directions on the compass rose?
   _____, _____, _____, and _____.

Name _____   Date _____

Making a Map

Directions

Make a map of your classroom. Remember to make a symbol for each object in the map key. Include a compass rose.

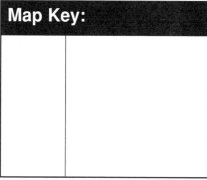

Map Key:

Answer Key

p. 9 Not necessarily in this order: countryside: wide, thing: swing, all: wall, brown: down, do: blue;

Not necessarily in this order: star: are, so: go, gone: upon, keep: peep, light: night, sky: eye, dark: spark

p. 13 Characters: Segi, mother, father, baby, Mimi; Setting: home, hospital; Problem: Segi didn't want to lose her parents' attention.; Events: Her mother is having a baby., Mimi tells her that her mother won't want to play with her.; Solution: Her mother tells her she will always be special.

Characters: Emma and her father, Setting: horse, hill, river; Problem: The horses got out and one crossed the river.; Events: Fence broke, horses escaped; Solution: Emma crossed the river, roped Belle, and led her across the river.

p. 16 Answers will vary.

p. 17 Make sure the words in each column are used in the five sections. Answers will vary

p. 20 Beginning: Reed went to Mandy's house.; They made sandwiches., They got out bread., Mandy put lettuce and cheese on one slice., Reed put on meat., They put the bread together., Mandy poured milk, and Reed got plates., End: They were ready to eat.

p. 22 Beginning: Jimmy invites Peter to play outside., They race to the tree., They throw the ball., They kick the ball., Jimmy shows Peter how to kick the ball high., End: They play until Jimmy has to do his homework.

p. 24 1. C: The children ate them., E: The cookies were gone.; 2. C: Billy's bike had a flat tire., E: He had to walk home.

p. 25 Not necessarily in this order: C: Jose was sick, E: He stayed home from school; C: Because nobody watered it, E: The plant died; C: Since it was Marie's birthday, E: She had a big cake; C: Emily raked the yard, E: She was given a dollar; C: Since it was raining, E: The children could not play outside.

p. 26 1. C: Jason and Chris were hot, E: they jumped into the water, 2. C: Molly lost her pencil, E: she had to buy another one, 3. C: it was hungry, E: Jenny fed her dog, 4. C: Alex left it out on the table, E: the ice cream melted.

p. 28 MI: Toys have been around for many years, but are very different today., D: earliest toys were very simple, there were dolls and animal toys, no moving parts, toys today can have many moving parts.

p. 29 MI: Winter is my favorite season of the year., D: I love to go sliding in the snow., I like to skate on the ice., I like to take walks on snowy nights., I like sitting by a warm fire and reading a book on a winter evening.

p. 30 MI: Terry wants to walk to school by himself., D: He is five., His mother wants him to wait until he is six., Terry tries to remember the safety rules., Every morning, he asks if he can walk to school by himself.

p. 33 S: Robert, W: to go fishing, B: his grandfather was taking too long to clean the garage, S: he helped him so they could go fishing. Summary: Robert wanted to go fishing, but his grandfather was taking too long to clean the garage, so he helped him so they could go fishing.

Peanut Pals: S: Maya, W: to make Chip her pet, B: Chip was not happy in the cage, S: she let him go. Summary: Maya wanted to make Chip her pet, but Chip was not happy in the cage, so she let him go.

p. 36

1. ◯ ⇨ , ABAB; 2. ▢ ◇ , AAB; 3. ▽ ▽ , AABB; 4. ☆ ▢ , ABB

p. 37

1. ABAB, ◯ ▭ ; 2. AAB, ▭ ▭ ; 3. AABB, ▢ ◯ ; 4. ABB, ▯ ;

5. ABAB, ▢ ▢

p. 38 Check patterns; answers will vary.

p. 40 6, 10, 14, 20, 22, 24, 28, 36, 40, 42, 44, 48, 50

p. 41 9, 15, 18, 24, 27, 33, 36, 42, 45, 54, 57

p. 42 1. 3, 5, 6, 8; 2. 5, 9, 13; 3. 6, 12, 14, 18, 20, 24, 28; 4. 7, 5, 3, 1; 5. 14, 10, 4, 2; 6. 15, 30, 45, 50, 60, 70

p. 44 1. Tom, 4, 2. 7 white tulips

p. 45 1. Lynn, 5 more, 2. 2 more

p. 46 4, 2, 4 − 2 = 2, Darius has 2 more yellow marbles than Delyn., 1. Brianna, 2. 2 more

p. 48 1–7. Check students' calendars., 8. Friday

p. 49 The calendar will vary each month.

p. 50 Answers will vary based on the calendar.

p. 52 1. Sphere, 2. Rectangular prism, 3. Cylinder, 4. Cube, 5. Cone.

p. 53 1. Cone, 2. Cube, 3. Cylinder, 4. Students will correctly match shapes.

p. 54 1. Students will accurately color the objects, 2. 5 spheres, 3 cubes, 8 cones, 5 cylinders, 7 rectangular prisms, 1 pyramid

p. 56 Guesses will vary, 1. 3, 2. 5, 3. 4, 4. 2

p. 57 Estimations and lengths will vary.

p. 58 For 1–3, check students' drawings, 4. Check students' measurements.

p. 60 Shade in 1 part on Window B; shade in 1 part on Window C.

p. 61 1. Shade 1 pane., 2. Shade 2 panes., 3. Shade 3 panes., 4. Shade 1 pane.

p. 62 1. Color 1 green, 2 yellow, 2. 2 orange, 1 red, 3. 2 blue, 3 orange, 4. 4 purple, 1 yellow, 5. 3 green, 1 purple, 6. 4 red, 2 blue, 7. Color 2 eggs.

p. 64 1. ice: solid, 2. water vapor: gas, 3. water: liquid

p. 65 1. solid, 2. liquid, 3. gas, 4. matter

p. 66 1. S, 2. L, 3. L, 4. G, 5. G, 6. S, 7. S, 8. L, 9. G

p. 68 Answers will vary.

p. 69 Answers will vary.

p. 70 1. temperature, 2. wind, 3. Sun, 4. clouds, 5. longer, 6. Fog, 7. water vapor

p. 72 Students draw pictures in the lowest level.

p. 73 Students color bottom row. They are in the bottom layer.

p. 74 See students' drawings.

p. 76 Students color the top, the sailboat, and the jet.

p. 77 Answers will vary.

p. 78 Check students' drawings.

p. 80 1. granite, 2. limestone, 3. pumice

p. 81 See students' pages for answers.

p. 82 Answers will vary.

p. 85 Compare the numbers with the students' graphs.

p. 86 Answers are dependent upon the students' graphs.

p. 89 Topic: Community, Larger details: people, buildings, businesses, restaurants. Small circles will vary.

p. 90 Students' answers will vary.

p. 93 1. north, 2. See pictures, 3. west, 4. east, 5. north, south, east, west

p. 94 Maps will vary. Check for map key and compass rose.